Airships Over North Channel

North Channel

Royal Naval Air Service Airships
in Ulster during the First World War

by Guy Warner

R.N. A.S.

Eric Lionel Warner and Martha Knox on their wedding day - both served at Larne naval base during the Great War

Guy Warner has been a regular contributor to Ulster Airmail, the journal of the Ulster Aviation Society for whom he is also a committe member.

As well as writing for *Aircraft Illustrated, Air Enthusiast, Air Pictorial, Aviation Ireland, Air International, Aviation News, History Ireland, Northern Ireland Travel News* and *230 Squadron Association Newsletter,* he has also had several books published.

He is co-author of *In the Heart of the City: The History of Belfast's City Airport, 1938–1998, Flying from Malone: Belfast's First Civil Aerodrome, Belfast International Airport: Aviation at Aldergrove since 1938, Army Aviation in Ulster* and author of *230 Squadron Royal Air Force.*

Guy is married with two daughters and lives in Co Antrim.

Designed by April Sky Design, Newtownards
www.aprilsky.co.uk

Foreword

Hitherto, only tantalising snippets of information about Bentra airship mooring-out station have been published and few historians have bothered to take more than a superficial interest. Indeed, prior to the appearance in 1981 of the late John Corlett's seminal work *Aviation in Ulster*, I like most people was unaware that such a facility had ever existed, let alone been the first military air base in Ulster. Shortly thereafter however, Bentra became an object of personal interest when I was asked by aviation historian Peter Connon to make some relevant enquiries in the Whitehead locality in connection with his researches into the aviation history of the Lake District and Dumfries & Galloway Region in neighbouring Great Britain. As a result, I was privileged to meet the late Miss Semple who, remarkably, was then living in the house at Larne Road, Whitehead immediately overlooking the site of the former Bentra mooring-out station. To my delight, in an album of photographs which she had inherited from her brother Jack she showed me numerous photographs taken at Bentra in 1917, three of which she graciously permitted me to copy for subsequent publication in Peter Connon's book *An Aeronautical History of the Cumbria, Dumfries and Galloway Region, Part 2: 1915 to 1930*.

My limited investigations on behalf of Peter Connon completed, my curiosity about Bentra was temporarily satisfied. At the time, I did not appreciate the full significance of the former air base or how important it had been in facilitating operations against German U-boats during the First World War. In that particular conflict, U-boats were employed on a potentially war-winning scale in terms of numbers and effectiveness, sinking about 5700 ships – 25% of the world's tonnage. Moreover, 70% of the sinkings occurred comparatively close to the coasts of Great Britain and Ireland. Notwithstanding the seemingly ineffective capabilities of the airships and aeroplanes then available to protect shipping, novel aerial techniques of anti-submarine warfare were nevertheless developed and a lot of crucial lessons were learned from hard experience, not least the importance of long range and endurance on the part of the aeroplanes and airships employed in that role. The fact that the political and military establishment failed to learn from those experiences (to the extent reflected by the inadequate tactics and strategies that were in place on the outbreak of the Second World War and were soon compelled to revise) simply underlines the fact that hard-won lessons of history must never be forgotten. To his credit, in *Airships Over The North Channel,* Guy Warner highlights the local and largely forgotten aspect of those germinal experiences which actually presaged the much more extensive and vital anti-submarine operations and training activities carried out from numerous bases in Northern Ireland during and indeed after the Second World War. I warmly congratulate him on this singular achievement and pay tribute to the amount of time, study and attention to detail he has put into the publication which is a comprehensive and fascinating account of the early development of one aspect of military aviation in Ulster during a very formative period in the wider history of such. I consider it a privilege that he invited me to write this foreword and afforded me the opportunity to play a tiny part in bringing his commendable work to fruition.

Happily, Jack Semple's album has survived and virtually all of the photographs in it relevant to the story of Bentra's airships are reproduced in the following pages, including the three originally made available to Peter Connon.

Ernie Cromie
Chairman Ulster Aviation Society

Author's Foreword

Eric Lionel Warner and Martha Knox both served at Larne Naval Base on the north-east coast of County Antrim during the First World War. My grandfather was an Englishman from Worcestershire and was a Marconi-trained wireless telegraphist who served all round the world in the merchant navy in the years before the war. He became a Commissioned Warrant Officer in the Royal Naval Reserve. After service in the armed merchant cruiser HMS *Macedonia*, in which he took part in the Battle of the Falkland Islands on 8th December 1914, he was posted to Larne as an instructor in wireless telegraphy. My grandmother was a country girl whose father was prominent in the Methodist Church at Ballynure. The family later moved to Station Road in Larne. During the war Martha joined the Women's Royal Naval Service - the Wrens. They met in the course of their duties and fell in love. After the war ended my grandfather was offered a permanent commission in the Royal Air Force. This he declined as he wished to stay in Larne and marry my grandmother - which they duly did on 25th October 1919 - remaining in the town for the rest of their long lives. They had two sons, my uncle Jim, born in 1921 and my father, Sam, who was born in 1924. This account is dedicated to their memory.

Grateful thanks are due to two airship experts, Ces Mowthorpe and Patrick Abbott, who have been most generous with their advice and with the loan of photographs. These have also been provided by Mrs Nancy Calwell, Donnie Nelson, Tom Jamison Ernie Cromie, Stuart Leslie, the Airship Heritage Trust, the Rolls-Royce Heritage Trust, Larne Borough Council, the U-Boat Archive and the Dover Museum. I am also greatly in the debt of the staff at the RAF Museum, the Imperial War Museum and the Fleet Air Arm Museum for their help. Thanks should also go to Michael Bradshaw for his technical advice and assistance. I must also record my appreciation of Norman Whitla's fine painting which graces the cover. Generous sponsorship has been received from the North Eastern Education and Library Board, Carrickfergus Borough Council, the Esme Mitchell Trust, the Lord O'Neill Charitable Trust, the Milibern Trust, Belfast International Airport, Ulster Local History Trust and the Larne & District Historical Society. As ever, this work would not have been possible without the forbearance and support of my wife, Lynda.

Guy Warner
Carrickfergus 2005

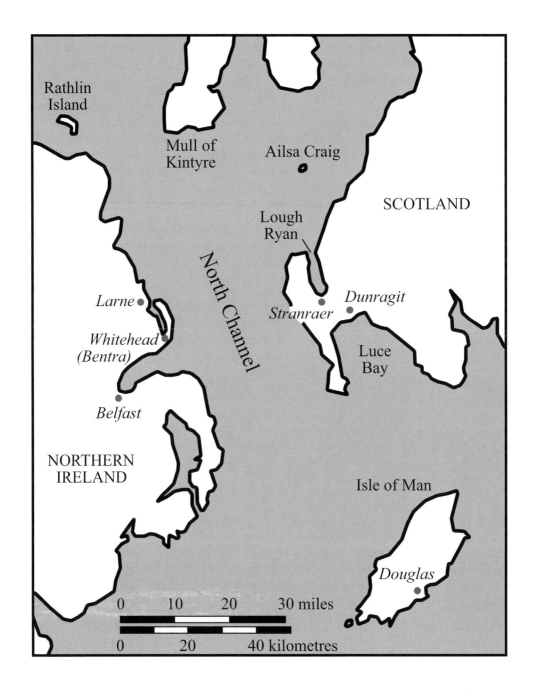

Rathlin
Island

Mull of
Kintyre

Ailsa Craig

SCOTLAND

Lough
Ryan

North Channel

Larne

*Whitehead
(Bentra)*

Stranraer

Dunragit

Luce
Bay

Belfast

NORTHERN
IRELAND

Isle of Man

Douglas

0	10	20	30 miles

0	20	40 kilometres

Background

The Great War of 1914-18 brought many technological innovations which served to add to the horror and carnage of the conflict. The war at sea was not immune from these developments as battle was engaged not only on the surface but also by underwater craft and in the air above. During the early months of the war attacks on warships of the Royal Navy by submarines or "U-boats" of the Imperial German Navy concentrated on the Grand Fleet in the waters near its anchorage at Scapa Flow in the Orkney Islands or along the east coast of Scotland where there was another naval base at Rosyth. However, as 1915 began, the area of hostile operations began to spread into the English Channel and the Irish Sea. In northern waters submarines were all but invisible when fully submerged, their presence given away only by oil patches on the surface. When at periscope depth and surveying the scene as they prowled below the waves, their position could then be betrayed by the distinctive but hard to spot (except from the air) "feathering" of the periscope through the water.

Larne

The port of Larne on the north-east coast of County Antrim was situated in a strategically important position on the North Channel between Ireland and Scotland, at the northern outlet of the Irish Sea where it meets the Atlantic Ocean. Any ship using the Western Approaches had to travel either to the north or south of Ireland. At that time, of

The position of a submarine given away by the feathering of its periscope through the water.
(Airship Heritage Trust)

The Princess Maud in Larne Harbour (Photograph reproduced by kind permission of Larne Borough Council Museum Service 2000.22.6)

course, all of Ireland was part of the United Kingdom. The sea route from Stranraer, at the head of Loch Ryan, to Larne was the shortest crossing between Great Britain and Ireland. From the very beginning of the war in August 1914, Larne increased in importance as a port for embarking and disembarking troops and supplies, as well as becoming a naval base in its own right. The Larne to Stranraer ferry service had been operated by the Larne and Stranraer Steamboat Company since 1872. It became the Portpatrick and Wigtownshire Railways Joint Committee in 1890. The *Princess Maud* was a handsome, two funnelled vessel of 1746 tons, constructed in 1904. Her companions, the *Princess May* and *Princess Victoria*, were requisitioned by the Admiralty, leaving the *Maud* to maintain this important lifeline on her own for the duration. Due to the threat likely to be imposed by hostile submarines and floating mines, countermeasures of a sort were taken from the start. Sailings were made at irregular times and route deviations were introduced sporadically. As Larne developed as a naval base, it became possible to provide an escort. The steamer, loaded with troops and sailors, would have been a fine kill, particularly when their numbers increased due to the development of a further naval base on Lough Swilly in County Donegal. The Olderfleet Hotel in Larne became a naval headquarters, under the direction of "Commodore Larne", Captain Carpendale. A sizeable fleet of armed trawlers and drifters, sturdy vessels for patrolling the sea lanes, began to assemble at the Naval Base. The route around the north coast down towards the Clyde and the Mersey was a fertile hunting ground. Anti-submarine nets were laid between Rathlin Island and the Scottish mainland, as well as at other points in the North Channel. These were maintained by the men of more than 200 craft based in Larne, which would play a role out of all proportion to their size and armament.

A fleet of trawlers and drifters similar to these were under the direction of Commodore Larne (Dover Museum)

Larne enters aviation history

Larne, the *Princess Maud* and the Olderfleet Hotel had entered aviation history only a bare year before the outbreak of the Great War. The Australian-born pioneer airman, Harry Hawker, had become the first aviator to cross the sea from Scotland to Ulster. He was taking part in a round-Britain flight for a prize of £5000 offered by the *Daily Mail*. His aircraft was a Sopwith HT (Hydro Tractor) Biplane Seaplane. On 27th August 1913 he flew from Oban to Larne Harbour, where he refuelled before setting out for Dublin. Hawker's arrival in Larne was fully reported in the *Larne Weekly Telegraph*, with some excellent photographs of the large, four-bay aircraft in the air and on the water. The paper reported, "As was only natural a number of people were early astir in Larne, this being the first visit of an air machine of any sort. It was 9.00 a.m. before the first glimpse was obtained and this was signalled from the Stranraer steamer *Princess Maud* which was lying just outside the lough. The noise of the siren was quickly followed by the sirens and whistles of all the craft lying in the harbour; and in a couple of minutes the machine was plainly visible to all. At first it appeared like a big bird on the horizon but quickly its proportions grew and it became evident that Hawker intended to descend immediately. A beautiful descent was made opposite the lighthouse at the entrance to Larne Lough and, on its floats, the huge machine swiftly passed through the narrow waterway to where the pilot boat was stationed. With the greatest ease the airmen made fast to a buoy just off the south pier in the bay, in front of the Olderfleet Hotel, amidst the delighted cheers of hundreds of spectators." For the next hour or more the two aviators (Hawker and his mechanic) were hard at work rectifying a choked engine oil pipe and replacing the spark plugs. He refused the proffered alcoholic beverages,

Harry Hawker and his aircraft on Larne Lough in 1913 (Photograph reproduced by kind permission of Larne Borough Council Museum Service DSC 0009)

saying that he was strictly TT but accepted a cigarette and some light refreshment. The newspaper continued, "In the meantime an immense crowd gathered on the pier head and on the various steamers to witness the novel sight. Scores of small boats plied hither and thither, making a circuit of the plane and hundreds availed themselves of this opportunity of seeing the novel craft at close quarters." Just before 11.00 a.m. the moorings were cast off, the engine set going and Hawker taxied about half a mile up Larne Lough before turning northwards into the wind, "quickly and gracefully it went up a distance of perhaps 100 feet. Rousing cheers greeted the intrepid aviator as his machine sailed overhead out of the Lough. It turned southwards and in a few minutes the aircraft was lost to view behind the Islandmagee hills." Further down the coast the aeroplane was observed over Whitehead crossing the mouth of Belfast Lough in the direction of Donaghadee. Spectators witnessed "the waterplane in full flight" from vantage points in Carrickfergus and Bangor. By 12.15 p.m. Hawker was passing over Ardglass.

Unfortunately mechanical problems induced a forced landing in the sea off the Irish coast at about 2.00 p.m. only thirteen miles from Dublin, in which the aeroplane was broken up, luckily without life-threatening injury to Hawker or his mechanic, H.Kauper. (Harry Hawker was the chief test pilot of the famous Sopwith Aviation Company throughout the First World War. He died in a flying accident in 1921 but his name lived on in Tom Sopwith's company which was renamed Hawker Aircraft Ltd.)

It was also noted in the *Larne Weekly Telegraph* that on Wednesday 27th August, "the observer of the Royal Army Aero Corps who had visited Islandmagee to select ground for the descent of the Army biplanes at present in Scotland paid a visit to Mr Hawker and proffered the assistance of mechanics etc." This was Captain George Dawes of No.2 Squadron, Royal Flying Corps (RFC), which was based at Montrose in Scotland.

The local press reported that he had selected a field on Islandmagee, near Larne, as being "suitable in every way for the brief occupation of the airmen". The town missed its chance to be part of this memorable event as "the commercial instincts of the owner of the land obviated the acceptance of the officer's terms, which were said to have been fairly liberal." Having been thus turned down, on 1st September 1913 the first overseas deployment of RFC took place between Castle Kennedy, near Stranraer and Rathbane Camp close to Limerick. Five B.E.2a aircraft and a single Maurice Farman Longhorn of 2 Squadron based at Montrose made the trip. Captain George Dawes, flying the Longhorn, became the first military aviator to land in Ulster when he broke his journey by alighting on the sands opposite the Slieve Donard Hotel, Newcastle, Co.Down at 1.50 p.m. on 1st September. This can be regarded as the dress rehearsal for the operational deployment of the air component of the BEF to France just under a year later.

One of those who greeted Hawker was Captain George Dawes RFC (JM Bruce/GS Leslie Collection)

The U-Boat war

After the repulse of the initial German advance and the establishment of a system of trenches running from Belgium to the Swiss border, the war in France had come to something of a stalemate. A decision was made to try and break the deadlock by the application of a change of tactics at sea. On 4th February 1915 a communiqué was issued by the Imperial German Admiralty which declared, "All the waters surrounding Great Britain and Ireland, including the whole of the English Channel, are hereby declared to be a war zone. From 18th February onwards every enemy merchant vessel found within this war zone will be destroyed without it always being possible to avoid danger to the crews and passengers. Neutral ships will also be exposed to danger in the war zone, as, in view of the misuse of neutral flags ordered on 31st January by the British Government, and owing to unforeseen incidents to which naval warfare is liable, it is impossible to avoid attacks being made on neutral ships in mistake for those of the enemy." This declaration opened the first phase of what was to become known as unrestricted submarine warfare. Restricted submarine warfare had meant the U-boat would surface, warn its intended victim, give the crew time to abandon ship and then sink it. Neutral cargo ships and all passenger liners, probably even Allied ones, would be spared.

Two U-boats (UB-82 and UB-89) of the Imperial German Navy prepare for sea (U-Boot Archiv)

In order not only to prosecute the war and to supply its troops with food and munitions but also to survive on the home front, Britain relied heavily on seaborne trade. If Germany could have broken or even seriously disrupted the flow of merchant vessels then Britain's ability to have waged war or indeed feed its population would have been rendered either difficult or impossible. Among the Royal Navy's many tasks were protecting trade, guarding the sea lanes and making safe the approaches to the major ports. Moreover, the German claim that unrestricted submarine warfare was justifiable was that it was a response to the Royal Navy's blockade of German shipping and any neutral vessels deemed to be carrying supplies useful to Germany. The tenuous nature of this claim can be challenged by considering the words of Admiral Reinhard Scheer, the last Commander-in-Chief of the High Seas Fleet, "The gravity of the situation demanded that we free ourselves of all scruples."

This was the nature of the problem facing the Admiralty under the political direction of the First Lord, Winston Churchill. However, as he recorded in his book, *The Great War*, the Admiralty was not too concerned at that stage. The Germans had moved too soon, there were simply not enough U-boats available in 1915 to make unrestricted submarine warfare any more than a considerable nuisance rather than a major threat. They compounded this error with a major miscalculation. On 7th May 1915, off the Irish coast, the British liner *Lusitania* was sunk by a single torpedo fired at a range of 700 yards by U-20, commanded by Kapitanleutnant Walther Schweiger. The great ship was destroyed in a sudden violent detonation (it was carrying a secret cargo of shells, ammunition and explosives) which resulted in the death of nearly 1200 of the 1600 souls on board. Over 100 of the dead were American citizens and such was the outcry that the Germans prudently scaled down the unrestricted nature of the submarine campaign in order to avoid incurring greater wrath from the USA.

Airship Development

To return to naval aeronautical matters, the Admiralty was not, however, unmindful of the potential threat posed by a greater submarine force. The professional head of the Royal Navy, the First Sea Lord, Admiral Lord Fisher, called a meeting at the Admiralty on 28th February 1915. He requested proposals to enhance the capability of the Navy to provide surveillance and deterrence from the air. He had in mind a small airship type to the following specification:

"(a) The airship was to search for submarines in enclosed or relatively enclosed waters.

(b) She was to be capable of remaining up in all ordinary weather, and should therefore have an air-speed of 40 to 50 m.p.h.

(c) She should have an endurance at full speed of about eight hours, carrying a crew of two.

(d) She should carry a wireless telegraphy outfit with a range of 30 to 40 miles.

(e) She should take up about 160 lbs. weight of explosives in the form of bombs.

(f) She should normally fly at about 750 feet altitude, but be capable of flying up to 5,000 feet.

(g) The design was to be as simple as possible, in order that large numbers of these ships should be produced without undue delay.

(h) An ample allowance of lift to be made for gas deterioration, so that each ship should remain in commission on one charge of gas as long as possible."

The new craft, which had been designated by Lord Fisher as submarine-searching or perhaps submarine-scout, would become known as the S.S. Class and would be crewed by the Royal Naval Air Service (RNAS).

The prototype S.S.Class airship took to the air within a month. The envelope of a small non-rigid airship, which had been in storage at Farnborough, was married with the fuselage of a B.E.2c aircraft. A non-rigid airship has no keel or metal framework, as was the case with the much larger Zeppelins. This is also known as a blimp.

A fabric envelope or gasbag filled with hydrogen was kept firm and in streamlined shape by internal air-filled bags or ballonets. As hydrogen is lighter than air it could carry the weight of the whole structure and its contents - the rule of thumb was that 1000 cubic feet of hydrogen would lift 65 lbs in weight. Beneath the gasbag was suspended a car which carried the crew, engine, fuel and weapons. The purpose of the engine was simply to push or pull the airship through the air, lift was not provided by forward movement generated by the engine but by the gas inside. The S.S.Class was a fairly simple and basic design but it had several merits. The production model met the specification as regards speed, 40-50mph, and endurance, 8-12 hours. It could climb with its crew of two to a height of more than 5000 feet. It was also cheap - with a unit cost of £2500. The shape was reasonably streamlined, being blunt at the nose but tapering towards the tail. The gasbag had a capacity of 60,000 cubic feet and was 143 feet six inches in length, with a maximum diameter of 27

General Arrangement of S.S. Airship (B.E.2c car)

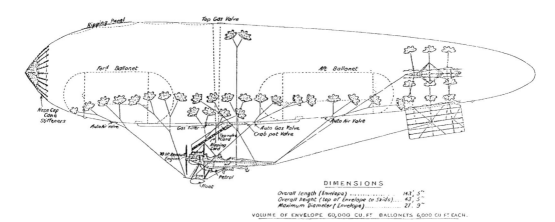

DIMENSIONS

Overall length (Envelope) .... 143' 5"
Overall height (top of Envelope to Skids)... 43' 5"
Maximum Diameter (Envelope)............. 27' 9"

VOLUME OF ENVELOPE 60,000 CU. FT BALLONETS 6,000 CU. FT EACH.

Above: The SS non-rigid blimps had two ballonets placed in tandem. The air was collected from the slipstream by a metal scoop and directed as required through manually operated valves into the ballonets, to maintain the internal pressure and so keep the envelope streamlined. Air could also be admitted selectively to control the trim; favouring one ballonet caused the airship to tilt.

Right: The utilisation of the propellor's slipstream to inflate the ballonets was a brilliantly simple solution to one of the main problems of non-rigid airship design. The method was devised for the SS prototype in 1915 and has since been used by nearly all British blimps up to the present day.

Blower Pipe and Valves on Smallest Type of Airship

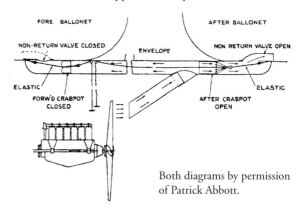

Both diagrams by permission of Patrick Abbott.

feet nine inches. (As a comparison this is about twice the length of a Shorts 360). The two internal ballonets mounted fore and aft not only ensured that the envelope kept its shape but could also be used by the pilot to adjust the airship's trim. They were inflated by means of a metal scoop mounted to catch the slipstream of the propeller. Two non-return valves made from fabric, the "crab-pots", controlled the flow of air into and out of the ballonets. The gross weight which the airship could lift including its own structure was 4180 lb, which gave a net lift available for crew, fuel, ballast and armament of 1434 lb. The disposable lift with a crew of two on board and full fuel tanks was 659 lb. The envelope was made of rubber-proofed fabric, reminiscent of an old-fashioned mackintosh. It consisted of four layers, two of fabric with a layer of rubber in between and on the inner surface. At the tail of the gasbag a single vertical fin and rudder were fitted ventrally, while horizontal fins and elevators were affixed to port and starboard.

To make it completely gastight and protected from the ravages of weather, salt water

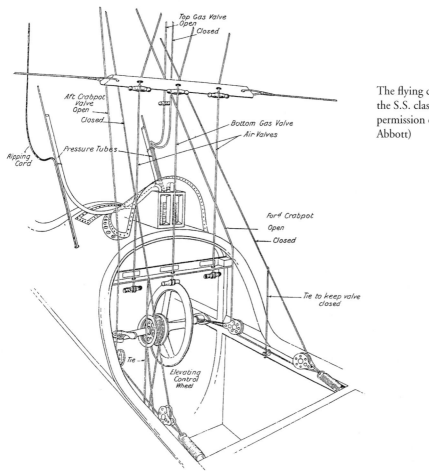

Labels in diagram:
- Top Gas Valve
- Open
- Closed
- Aft Crabpot Valve
- Open
- Closed
- Bottom Gas Valve
- Air Valves
- Pressure Tubes
- Ripping Cord
- Ford Crabpot
- Open
- Closed
- Tie to keep valve closed
- Tie
- Elevating Control Wheel

The flying controls of the S.S. class airship (by permission of Patrick Abbott)

and sun, four coats of dope were applied to the outer surface, with a top coat being of aluminium varnish. The B.E.2c fuselage was retained stripped of its wings, rudder, elevators and eventually wheels, axles and suspension.

Propulsion was by means of a 75 hp air-cooled Renault engine driving a large four-bladed propeller. The observer, who also operated the wireless set, sat in the front seat with the pilot behind him. It was powered by two four volt accumulator batteries rather than by fitting a generator driven by the engine. This had two advantages, it was lighter and would still operate in the event of an engine failure. Communication was by means of Morse Code. The wireless telegraphy receiver and Type 52 transmitter had a range of between 50 and 60 miles, when flying at not less than 800 feet. A long trailing aerial some 200 feet in length with a lead weight on the end to keep it from fouling any part of the airship was wound down from a reel fitted to the side of the car. Small bombs, eight 16 lb. or two 65 lb. and a Lewis machine-gun could be carried by way of armament. A lever bomb-sight was fitted and the release was operated by Bowden wire control. It was considered to be, "capable of being flown by a young midshipman with small-boat training". To this end junior officers were brought in from the Grand Fleet by means of ships' Captains being asked to select midshipmen willing to volunteer for "special temporary and hazardous service." One of these was Thomas Elmhirst, from the battlecruiser HMS *Indomitable*, whom we shall meet shortly. Enthusiastic, young, direct entry civilians were also induced to join up - specifically for this purpose. An intensive training course, lasting about a month, was given in the theory of aerostatics (aeronautics, navigation, meteorology, engineering, rigging and engine overhaul), practical balloon flying and mastering the controls of a small airship. The young officers greatly enjoyed the balloon flying, eight qualifying flights - six under instruction (including a night flight), one trip as second in command and finally, a solo. Elmhirst's solo was in Suffolk when the only difficulty encountered was, after landing in a thorn hedge, when an inquisitive local with a smoking pipe in his mouth began to examine closely the gas valve aperture. He was dissuaded from this dangerous practice very quickly.

Admiral Fisher demanded that forty more of these small airships should be produced as expeditiously as possible. Neither the First Sea Lord nor the First Lord were to remain at the Admiralty long enough to see the S.S. Class into operation. In May, following the tragedy of the Dardanelles Campaign, Winston Churchill resigned and Jackie Fisher also departed. They were succeeded by the former Prime Minister, Arthur Balfour and Admiral Sir Henry Jackson, respectively.

Luce Bay

Aerial surveillance would also play a part in the naval activities controlled by "Commodore Larne". In the spring of 1915 an airship base was constructed at Luce Bay in Wigtownshire, on the coast of Dumfries and Galloway, four and a half miles south-east of Stranraer. It was organised on naval lines, with a small parade ground carefully surrounded by whitewashed stones and referred to as the "Quarterdeck", a ship's bell and a flag-staff flying the White Ensign. At some distance from the accommodation and offices the land fell away in a gentle slope to the landing ground on which stood the airship shed, the gas-plant, tanks and power house. The shed was a lofty and substantial structure constructed of corrugated iron, lit rather dimly by a row of windows in the upper part of the walls. It was guarded at all times by a sentry whose task was to ensure that no smoking materials were taken inside. These were deposited in a cupboard to be reclaimed later. This was a very sensible precaution owing to the proximity of large quantities of hydrogen. It could hold up to four of the new S.S.Class. Beyond the shed lay a stretch of marshland and sand dunes around the bay. At the beginning of August the first S.S.Class airships were brought to the little station at Dunragit by rail and then seven miles by road through winding lanes flanked by tall hedges or grassy banks for inflation on site at Luce Bay. They were S.S.17 and S.S.23. The next arrival was flown in on 17th August, S.S.20. They were secured in the shed by means of wire mooring cables, allowing the gas-filled envelopes to sway gently in the draught created when the sliding main doors were opened. The first operational flight from Luce Bay took place on 23rd August. It was a one hour patrol over the North Channel in S.S.17 made by Flight Sub-Lieutenant T.W.Elmhirst.

An aerial photograph of RNAS Luce Bay, note the airship to the right of the picture (JM Bruce/GS Leslie Collection)

The view from an airship approaching Loch Ryan and the familiar landmark of the lighthouse on Corsewall Point (Donnie Nelson Collection)

Piloted by Flt Sub-Lt TW Elmhirst, S.S.17 takes to the air at Barrow on 3rd July 1915, it was the first Vickers-built airship to fly and was sent to RNAS Luce Bay by rail. (Ces Mowthorpe via JM Bruce/GS Leslie Collection)

Flt Sub-Lt TP Yorke-Moore (centre cockpit) about to take an instructional flight in S.S.23 (Donnie Nelson Collection)

S.S.23, piloted by Flt Sub-Lt TP Yorke-Moore, approaches over Torrs Warren prior to landing at Luce Bay (Donnie Nelson Collection)

S.S.20 prepares to land at Luce Bay in 1915 (Ces Mowthorpe Collection)

The first crossing to Ireland by airship

The next incident of note took place not long afterwards when Elmhirst had a very unpleasant experience in S.S.17. The rudder controls of the airship failed over the North Channel, rendering it as subject to the whims of the wind as a balloon. The wind was blowing easterly and off-shore, conditions were very bumpy. As the airship drifted towards the Irish coast, Elmhirst alighted on the water close to a trawler, whose skipper he asked for help. The crew simply ignored his entreaties. Even worse the propeller blades had touched the sea and had broken, forcing Elmhirst to switch off the engine. Ascending again the S.S.17 was blown towards another fishing vessel. Descending once more no helpful response ensued. With all its water ballast gone the airship was in a perilous position, so Elmhirst and his observer threw anything removable overboard, including the bombs, radio set and compass - to gain as much height as possible. A 40 lb bag of sand ballast, the grapnel and its long trailing rope were the last to go over the side. By this means it was possible to climb over the 300 feet high sheer cliffs to the north of Larne and to make a landing by pulling on the ripcord to totally deflate the envelope. A local farmer and his wife helped the aviators to un-rig and pack up the downed craft and then provided very welcome refreshments. The Senior Naval Officer sent a couple of lorries to collect them but gave them rather a grumpy greeting in comparison to the farmer and his wife. "Commodore Larne" subsequently asked the trawler captains just why they had been so unhelpful. The reply came, "We did observe a British airship manoeuvring; it was a very pretty sight.", which may give some clue as to their political sympathies. Be as that may, Elmhirst was to assert later that he had made the first crossing from Great Britain to Ireland by airship (a balloon had first made the journey across the Irish Sea on 18 July 1817, by which means Windham Sadler was carried from Dublin to Holyhead).

By September, long airship patrols to the Irish coast were being made. Progress was hindered by a spate of forced landings due to trouble with the temperamental engines.

Bentra

Consideration was given to what Luce Bay based airships would do in the event that unfavourable weather prevented returning to base. A mooring out station was established at Whitehead, at the head of Larne Lough, some eight miles south of Larne. This may be dated from the fact that a bank account was opened in the name of the RNAS at the Northern Bank in Whitehead on 14th October 1915, under the authorised signature of the Officer Commanding, Sub-Lieutenant Archibald Creighton. The land belonged to a local farmer, James Long of Bentra, a mile and a quarter out of the little seaside town of Whitehead.

The flight of H.M.A.No.4

The residents of the town were able to have sight of a much larger airship on 3rd November 1915 when H.M.A.No.4, under the command of Flight Lieutenant

Above and below: An airship lands at Bentra, Whitehead (D&N Calwell Collection)

H.M.A.No.4 takes to the air (JM Bruce/GS Leslie Collection)

F.L.M.Boothby flew directly from Walney Island, near Barrow-in-Furness, to the County Antrim coast. This non-rigid airship, which had been ordered before the war by the Admiralty from the German Parseval company, had a cubic capacity six times greater than the S.S.Class. It carried a crew of nine in a roomy open car made from duralumin and was powered by two 170 hp Maybach engines. During the autumn of 1915 it made several training and proving flights as far as north-east Antrim, the Mull of Galloway, the Isle of Man and Anglesey.

From the end of 1915 to the start of 1917

The winter months of 1915-16 brought very poor weather which greatly hindered the fledgling operation at Luce Bay and considerably reduced the possibility of making any patrols at all. By early 1916 the station had a naval complement of about 40, half of whom were officers. HM Motorboat No.8 was based nearby at Drummore and was used mostly for target towing and local off-shore patrols. It was not until the middle of March 1916 that any serious aerial activity resumed. This coincided with the arrival of two more airships, S.S.33 and S.S.38. These were different in that their cars resembled the fuselage of a Maurice Farman aeroplane and were fitted with pusher rather than tractor propellers - which had the advantage of enabling the crew to avoid buffeting from the slipstream. They were slightly slower than the B.E.2c models but the cars were somewhat roomier and more comfortable for the crew. The pilot sat in the front seat, with the wireless telegraphy operator/observer behind. Dual flying controls were provided. A third seat could be installed for a passenger or engineer. Engine reliability was a problem with the S.S. Class,

The configuration of the Maurice Farman type fuselage is clearly shown in this picture (Airship Heritage Trust)

S.S.30A at Cranwell in 1918, a good close-up of the Maurice Farman car (Ces Mowthorpe Collection)

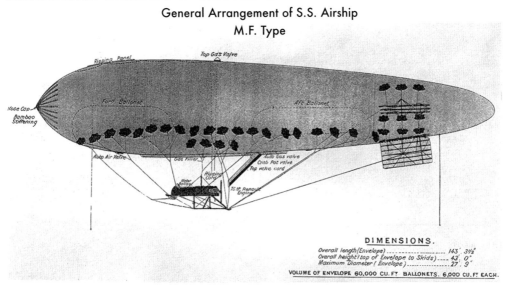

General Arrangement of S.S. Airship
M.F. Type

DIMENSIONS.

Overall length (Envelope) .... 143' 3½"
Overall height / top of Envelope to Skids) .... 43' 0"
Maximum Diameter (Envelope) .... 27' 9"

VOLUME OF ENVELOPE 60,000 CU. FT   BALLONETS. 6,000 CU. FT EACH.

A plan drawing of the S.S. Class airship - Maurice Farman car (Guy Warner Collection)

faulty cylinder heads being a particular problem. At times running repairs were even carried out in flight, standing on the skids, holding on with one hand while working with the other. Unbelievable as it now sounds, the engine was then restarted by a hefty swing on the propeller.

The oldest airship, S.S.17, had been relegated to training duties since September 1915 and was deflated in April before being sent to Wormwood Scrubs Depot. It is of interest to note that activities were also curtailed by the fact that the crew of the *Princess Maud* was on strike for most of April, owing to a wages dispute. Patrols continued over the summer months but at a fairly low level. Sometimes an airship on early patrol would return with a supply of fish for breakfast. The pilot would maintain station over a fishing vessel and let down a basket containing tobacco or newspapers on the end of the wireless aerial. The fishermen would trade these for a welcome dietary supplement. On one occasion a pilot was returning with a laden basket when fog descended on the landing ground. In the gloom he managed to scrape the roof of the CO's house with the result that the fishy cargo was spilt over the side. Quite how the CO reacted to this "manna from heaven" landing in his garden has not been recorded.

Flying the SS Class

It is hard to imagine now just what it would have been like for the crews of the Submarine Scout airships, suspended in an open cockpit, between a few hundred and a few thousand feet above the cold, grey sea, making slow headway against the wind. Luckily two such pilots recorded their impressions. Air Marshal Sir Thomas Elmhirst recalled his experiences as a young pilot of only 19 years of age, "I controlled height by means of a wheel in my right hand linked by wires to elevator planes stuck on the after end of the

gasbag and direction by foot pedals again connected by wires to a rudder at the after end of the gasbag. My other controls, to be operated by the left hand, were the engine, the gas valve, two ballonet air valves and an air pressure control cable. I had a red cord to rip the top off the gasbag in case of a forced landing and a handpump to top up the main fuel tank under my seat from the gravity feed tank for the engine. I had made a wooden bomb sight - quite simply two nails as foresight and backsight, the foresight being moveable to a scale marked with the speed of approach, 20 to 50 knots. My other instruments were mounted on a board to the front of the cockpit - a watch, air-speed and height indicators, an engine revolution counter, an inclinometer, gas, oil and petrol pressure gauges and a glass petrol level indicator. These all had to be monitored closely. Provision was made for illuminating the instruments by four small bulbs. Navigation was by means of chart and floor-mounted compass. A map case with a celluloid front formed the door to a small cupboard." Whilst doing all of this he also had to pass messages back and forth to his wireless operator, read his maps, take compass bearings, plot his course and at the same time keep a constant watch on the sea below. It should be noted that conditions were cramped and confined on board, exposed to the cold and at the mercy of the elements - the speed through the air of these craft could be reduced to only a few knots when flying into a head-wind. This would be not be a pleasant experience when returning from a long patrol - tired, hungry and cold. Another airship pilot of the period, T.B. Williams, wrote, "As the pilot could not leave his little bucket seat during a flight of often many hours duration, he just didn't get a meal. It

Another aerial view of Luce Bay, this time taken from S.S.20, flown by Flt Cdr Hartford on 17th June 1917 (Donnie Nelson Collection)

was also difficult to answer the call of nature. I evolved an arrangement made up from a petrol funnel to which was attached a piece of rubber hose passing to a water tight junction in the hull under my seat. The petrol funnel was hung on a brass cup hook near my elbow. I had some difficulty in inventing a purpose for this gadget when explaining the instruments and controls to the wife of a VIP on one occasion."

The Commanding Officer at Luce Bay, Flight Commander G.C.Colmore must have visited Whitehead from time to time, as in September 1916 his name was added to the list of authorised signatures for cheques at the local bank. George Colmore had gained his Royal Aero Club Aviators' Certificate on 21st June 1910, being awarded No.15 (just before Captain George Dawes, who received No.17 a month later). Colmore handed over command of Luce Bay to Flight Commander I.H.B.Hartford on 1st November 1916, whose name was duly inscribed in the Northern Bank's ledger five days later.

As the year wore on into the autumn and winter all was fairly quiet, with enemy action being confined to an area around the Isle of Man. Life at Luce Bay was rather pleasant, discipline was not oppressive. When flying was not possible owing to the Scottish climate, personnel enjoyed the navy tradition of a "make and mend" day. Huts for the men were exceptionally comfortable with washing facilities and a bathroom, rather than a communal washhouse. The officers and their servants enjoyed being billeted in a nearby requisitioned country residence, Dunragit House. However, much was to change in the next few months.

The log of S.S.20 records that Flight Commander Hartford flew as far as Larne on 16th January and returned overhead the rocky volcanic mound of Ailsa Craig (otherwise known as Paddy's Milestone and then as now a convenient navigational feature). The following day the weather was favourable enough to allow another aerial visit to Larne Harbour, which no doubt was appreciated by the townsfolk and naval base personnel. There is no record of this or indeed of any other wartime naval activity in the *Larne Weekly Times*, doubtless due to the restrictions imposed by censorship which saw the suspension of the publication of synoptic weather charts in the press, lest valuable information reached the enemy by this means. Larne was visited once more on 13th February. No landings on Irish soil were recorded.

Unrestricted submarine warfare recommences

On 1st February 1917 the Imperial German Government declared the resumption of unrestricted submarine warfare. U-boats were available in quantity and this time not only allied shipping but also neutral vessels (such as those on the US register) would be sunk on sight in the eastern Atlantic and the approaches to British ports. This was an enormous gamble, America would inevitably enter the war (the USA declared war on Germany on 6th April 1917) but could the Allies be starved into submission before sufficient reinforcements and materiel could arrive to break the deadlock on the Western Front? The Chancellor, Bethmann-Hollweg assessed the situation facing the Germans, "On the whole, the prospects for the unrestricted U-boat war are very favourable. Of course, it must be admitted that those prospects are not capable of being demonstrated by proof. We should be perfectly certain that, so far as the military situation is concerned, great military strokes are insufficient as such to win the war. The U-boat war is the 'last card'. A very serious decision. But if the military authorities consider the U-boat war essential, I am not in a position to contradict them."

The initial impact cannot be understated. In the first three months, over 1000 merchant ships were sunk. The situation was perilous. Winston Churchill later wrote, "At first sight all seemed to favour the Germans. Two hundred U-boats each possessing between three and four weeks' radius of action, each capable of sinking with torpedo, gun fire or bomb, four or five vessels in a single day, beset the approaches to our islands along which passed in and out every week several thousand merchant vessels. Of all the tasks ever set to a Navy none could have appeared more baffling than that of protecting this enormous traffic and groping deep below the surface of the sea for the deadly elusive foe. It was in fact a game of Blind Man's Buff in an unlimited space of three dimensions."

The government minister charged with responsibility for taking action at this time of crisis, the First Lord of the Admiralty, was a politician well-known in Ireland, Sir Edward Carson. Much debate ensued within the Admiralty as to the most appropriate type of countermeasures. In the end it was realised that grouping merchant ships into convoys escorted by naval vessels and naval airships was the most effective form of protection. This was put into effect from May 1917.

S.S.20 in the airship shed at Bentra (D&N Calwell Collection)

Developments at Bentra

During the course of a Western Patrol, Flight Commander Hartford landed at Whitehead twice on 7th April, flying S.S.20, at 1pm and again at 3pm. Flight Sub-Lieutenant A.V.Pullan made a similar stop on 3rd May. The facilities there were being improved to enable the mooring out station to make a greater contribution in the light of the highly increased threat. Ditches were filled in. A portable airship shed was erected, consisting of a steel frame covered by canvas, measuring 150 feet long by 45 feet wide and 50 feet high. Wooden huts on brick and concrete foundations were built to act as accommodation on site. The primary task for the airship making its way to Bentra early each morning was to escort the *Princess Maud*. Around midday, when the prevailing wind was often unfavourable, the airship could be housed, ready to take to the air again in the evening when the wind dropped. The introduction of the convoy system brought fresh duties, scouting for submarines on the surface or the wake of a periscope. Co-operation between naval airmen and the warships below was of the highest importance. Every hour the airship would transmit its call sign and so allow its position to be plotted by cross bearings from strategically placed wireless stations. If anything suspicious was sighted then warships could be directed to the precise location without delay. An airship could take position to windward of a convoy and could swoop down fairly quickly to investigate a possible threat at a speed nearly twice that which a destroyer could achieve. It could receive messages by Aldis lamp from escorting warships and it could scout ahead for mines - which could be detonated by machine-gun fire.

Both doors open, an airship can clearly be seen inside the shed (D&N Calwell Collection)

An airship emerges from the shed (D&N Calwell Collection)

The ground crew pose for a photograph in front of the shed (D&N Calwell Collection)

S.S.23 is prepared for flight from Bentra (D&N Calwell Collection)

S.S.23 landed at Bentra, note James Long's farmhouse to the right and Muldersleigh Hill in the background (D&N Calwell Collection)

The first airship to use the shed at Whitehead was S.S.20 on 5th June, flown by Flight Sub-Lieutenant W.E.C.Parry. He encountered some rough weather while on a routine flight and had made for shelter. He had to stay there for four days until the conditions improved, returning to Luce Bay after a Western Patrol on 9th June. That evening Flight Commander Hartford made another three hour Western Patrol, landing at Whitehead to pick up Air Mechanic Futcher. On 10th June S.S.20 returned to Whitehead, flown by Flight Sub-Lieutenant Chambers and spent eight hours on the ground there between patrols. Soon afterwards Pullan in S.S.23 experienced engine trouble and was able to find a safe haven there as well. On 11th June Flight Commander Hartford flew to Bentra, bringing with him an engineer to repair S.S.23's engine. This happened again in early July with Flight Commander Hartford coming across once more. However, changes were afoot - S.S.20 and S.S.35 had been inspected by the Admiralty Board of Survey and condemned as being unfit for service. S.S.24 had flown up from RNAS Anglesey to take on some of the burden but a much greater augmentation was at hand - the first of the new S.S.Z. Class to arrive at Luce Bay for inflation had also arrived. Before the end of July both S.S.Z.11 and S.S.Z.12 had made their first operational patrols from Luce Bay. They were joined by S.S.Z.13 in August. Of the older S.S.type only S.S.23 remained.

Departure of S.S.Z.12 from Bentra (D&N Calwell Collection)

The S.S.Z.Class

The S.S.Zero was built to the design of three RNAS officers. The car was specifically designed to be streamlined in shape and was constructed almost like a boat, with a keel and ribs of wood with curved longitudinal members. The whole frame was braced with piano wire and then floored from end to end. It was enclosed with 8-ply wood covered with aluminium. The crew of three consisted of the wireless telegraphist/observer/gunner in the front, with the pilot in the middle and the engineer in his own compartment to the rear. A machine-gun could be mounted either to port or starboard, operated from the front seat and two 110 lb bombs could be carried. The car, as well as being boat-shaped, was watertight so the airship could land on calm water. It was powered by a 75 hp Rolls-Royce Hawk six-cylinder, vertical in-line, water-cooled engine driving a four-bladed pusher propeller. 200 of these were manufactured under licence by Brazil Straker of Bristol, which was the only company entrusted by Henry Royce to build complete engines. It was a superb creation and was test run for the first time at the end of 1915. The words of an airship pilot tell it all, "The sweetest engine ever run - it only stops when switched off or out of petrol." It gave the airship a top speed of 53 mph and a rate of climb of 1200 feet per minute. Slung on either side of the gasbag were two petrol tanks made from aluminium. The gasbag had a capacity of 70,000 cubic feet. It was of the same length as the S.S. Class gasbag but was of a slightly greater diameter. The nose of the gasbag was reinforced by radially positioned canes to prevent it buckling at speed. As with the S.S. Class it was attached to the car with cables secured to the envelope by kidney-shaped "Eta" adhesive patches, which were also sown on,

The car of the S.S.Z. class airship was streamlined and boat-shaped (Rolls-Royce Heritage Trust)

An S.S.Z. class airship is prepared for flight (Rolls-Royce Heritage Trust)

An S.S.Z. class airship is being hauled down (in this case at RNAS Pembroke in 1917). The trail-rope is in the hands of the handling party, the engine is stopped and the engineer is standing while switching everything off (Ces Mowthorpe Collection)

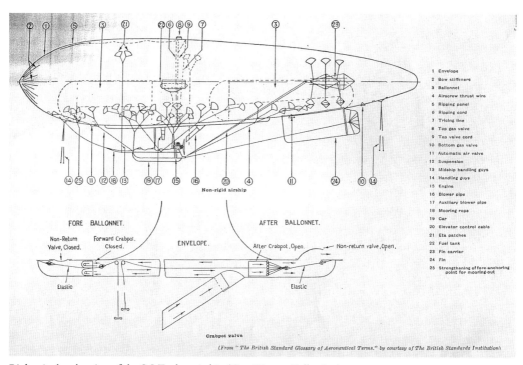

1	Envelope
2	Bow stiffeners
3	Ballonnet
4	Airscrew thrust wire
5	Ripping panel
6	Ripping cord
7	Tricing line
8	Top gas valve
9	Top valve cord
10	Bottom gas valve
11	Automatic air valve
12	Suspension
13	Midship handling guys
14	Handling guys
15	Engine
16	Blower pipe
17	Auxiliary blower pipe
18	Mooring rope
19	Car
20	Elevator control cable
21	Eta patches
22	Fuel tank
23	Fin carrier
24	Fin
25	Strengthening of fore-anchoring point for mooring-out

Non-rigid airship

FORE BALLONNET.

Non-Return Valve, Closed.   Forward Crabpot, Closed.

AFTER BALLONNET.

ENVELOPE.

After Crabpot, Open.   Non-return valve, Open.

Elastic   Elastic

Crabpot valve

(From "The British Standard Glossary of Aeronautical Terms," by courtesy of The British Standards Institution)

Right: A plan drawing of the S.S.Z. class airship (Guy Warner Collection)

The Rolls-Royce Hawk - "the sweetest engine ever run" (Rolls-Royce Heritage Trust)

so spreading the load evenly. The S.S.Z.s or Zeros as they were known, were more stable in flight than the S.S.Class and had much greater endurance. They were able to fly in weather conditions that would have prevented the earlier type from operating. The unit cost was about £5000.

The arrival of the more capable S.S.Z.s and the greater flexibility allowed by the erection of the shed at Whitehead ensured that September was a very busy month with regard to patrols, training and test flights.

Excitement at Whitehead

It must have been particularly exciting that summer of 1917 for the children of what is, even today, a quiet country district. What must they have felt seeing a strange craft descending from the sky with its helmeted, goggled and muffled crews? Fortunately an eye-witness to these times has spoken to the author, Mrs Nancy Calwell (back then Nancy Wisnon), who was a young girl six years of age, living near Bentra. Her uncle was James Long, the farmer who owned the land. When the drone of an airship's engine could be heard approaching, the local children would run down the side of the adjacent field to watch through the hedge. A photograph has survived of Nancy and her friends peering over

S.S.Z.11, landed at Bentra under the watchful gaze of Nancy and her friends (D&N Calwell Collection)

a gate in awe at the sight which they beheld. Soon Nancy was adopted as a mascot by the airmen and given sweets and chocolate. One day in particular she was given a never to be forgotten treat. An airship was coming in to land, as usual nose to wind. The pilot threw down a rope for the mooring party of naval personnel, farmers and labourers to grab hold of. When it drew closer to the ground they could reach up for the guy-ropes attached to the bows and the stern. When it was close enough to the ground, Nancy was lifted into the cockpit onto the pilot's knee. The landing party moved forward tugging on the ropes to "walk" the airship into the shed (which also saw use as an extra hay barn). Nancy was flying a few feet above the ground and could dream of being an airship pilot ranging out over the sea.

Handling on the ground could be a tricky business as an airship presented a sizeable bulk to the wind and was naturally buoyant in this element. When safely in the shed maintenance could be carried out by the riggers and mechanics, with their patches, rubber solution and dope. For take-off the airship would be made positively buoyant so that it could be "walked" out of the shed. Trim would be checked, the engine started, the order to "Let go" would be given and the craft would rise gently into the wind.

U-Boat successes

October brought successful U-boat attacks on the cruiser H.M.S. *Drake* and the S.S. *Main* off the Antrim and Galloway coasts respectively. Flight Commander Hartford responded with an increased level of aerial activity despite poor weather and gale force winds. Later in the month "Commodore Larne" requested that an airship be sent to search

S.S.Z.20 on the ground (JM Bruce/GS Leslie Collection)

for mines reported to be floating off the coast. A fourth S.S.Z. was ready, S.S.Z.20, with the result that S.S.23 was taken out of service, her last flight being the return from Bentra on 31st October in the hands of Flight Sub-Lieutenant Pullan. The weather in November continued to be poor - on 25th strong winds gusting to 73 mph tore apart the canvas door curtains of the Whitehead shed. Winds of this velocity are tabulated on the Beaufort Scale as Force 11 to 12, which equates to a violent storm or hurricane. There was a danger that the airship sheltering inside would be carried away or badly damaged. A telephone call brought the army to the rescue in horse-drawn wagons. After helping to make everything secure, they "ate up the available rations and departed". The shed was unusable for nearly a month until a sailmaker could be flown over to effect repairs. A high level of enemy activity continued - helped by often atrocious weather. Reports of sinkings, near misses and running battles between merchant ships and U-boats poured into the operations offices at Luce Bay and in Larne. The war came even closer to Whitehead on 28th December 1917 when the Elders and Fyffes liner *Chirripo* of 4050 tons was sunk by a mine about half a mile south-east of the cliffs at Black Head, which was on the far slope of Muldersleigh Hill from Bentra. 1917 ended with four S.S.Z. airships in commission at Luce Bay. The number of personnel at the base had by this time expanded to about 170.

The combination of adverse weather and intense enemy action continued unabated into the New Year. On 26th February another ship went down off Black Head, the Anchor Line *Tiberia* of 4880 tons, which was torpedoed. A peak was reached in March 1918 when no less than 65 patrols were flown during the month. A new pilot had arrived in February,

An airship pilot needed protection from the elements. It is believed that this photo was taken by Flt Sub Lt Bert Crump (via Tom Jamison)

Flight Sub-Lieutenant A.H.Crump, who was just nineteen years old and had been described as "an exceptionally good lad" by the District Coastwatching Officer when serving on Coastguard patrol duties as a Sea Scout in 1915. Fortunately his Flying Log Book has survived to give an insight into the duties of the airship crews in the final months of the war. After five hours of training in the capable hands of Flight Commander Hartford and Flight Lieutenant Pullan, to familarise him with the area, Bert Crump made his first operational patrol from Luce Bay in S.S.Z.20 on 25th February, escorting a convoy for seven hours and 35 minutes.

Engine trouble afflicted Flight Lieutenant Pullan again on 3rd March, when he had to land S.S.Z.12 at Bentra for repairs. The following day Flight Sub-Lieutenant Crump

An S.S.Z. class airship, looking over the pilot's head to the engineer's station at the rear of the car.
(via Tom Jamison)

carried out an 11 hour patrol in S.S.Z.13 which included escorting the *Princess Maud* - a duty which he was to repeat more than once over the next few months. The first bomb to be dropped in anger from a Luce Bay airship was on 17th March (St.Patrick's Day) when S.S.Z.11 flown by Flight Sub-Lieutenant S.B.Harris attacked a suspected submarine off the Copeland Islands at the mouth of the south side of Belfast Lough. Harris made another bombing attack before the end of the month while escorting a north-bound convoy near the entrance of Belfast Lough.

Avro 504s were manufactured by Harland and Wolff in Belfast (via Ernie Cromie)

An unusual cargo

A most unusual escort duty took place on 29th March 1918, when an airship accompanied the *Princess Maud* bearing a unique cargo from Larne to Stranraer. The story had begun some six months earlier, in August 1917, when the War Cabinet authorised the Handley Page Company (H.P.) to construct three prototypes of a large strategic bomber, even bigger than its O/100 and O/400 twin-engine heavy bombers. As the H.P. factory in Cricklewood in North London was working to full capacity, it was decided to make use of the expert draughtsmen, carpenters and fitters of the shipbuilders, Harland and Wolff Ltd., in Belfast. To this end, the Chief Designer, G.R.Volkert, went there to take charge of the project at the head of a team from H.P., while Frederick Handley Page himself visited the city every weekend to monitor progress (returning to London by means of the *Princess Maud* and the railway from Stranraer on Mondays with all the Ulster ham and bacon he could carry).

Harland and Wolff also already had relevant experience in aircraft manufacture, having commenced in 1916 the construction of an eventual total of nearly 1000 single engine D.H.6s and Avro 504s, which were shipped by water to England.

On 28th February 1918, Aldergrove in County Antrim was selected as the site for the flying test field for the new bomber, with the result that the construction of final assembly hangars was needed. The flight sheds were not ready in time for the first prototype. So the massive H.P. V/1500 was transported in parts to Cricklewood (the fuselage was shipped

The Handley Page V/1500 was flown from Aldergrove as well as being sent by sea (Ernie Cromie Collection)

directly to London from Belfast but the 2800 square feet wings went by way of the *Princess Maud* from Larne and then by rail to Euston) where it flew for the first time, registered as B9463, on 22nd May 1918.

From the RNAS to the RAF

Meanwhile, on 31st March 1918 came the final patrols by personnel of the RNAS. From the following morning they were conducted by those of the Royal Air Force (RAF). They were the same crews but the RNAS and the Royal Flying Corps (RFC) had merged to form the RAF. One significant change was the adoption of military ranks. Another was the closure of the bank account at Whitehead in the name of the RNAS on 17th April, the final authorised signature being that of Assistant Paymaster G.R.Renniser, who had taken over this administrative function from Flight Commander Hartford in January.

Oddly enough, the Admiralty retained responsibility for the actual airships until October 1919. Patrol and escort duties continued with two more notable landings at Bentra. On 9th April, Lieutenant Pullan had to land

Lt Pullan was a regular visitor to Bentra (D&N Calwell Collection)

43

Light naval forces combined to fight the UB-85 (Dover Museum)

S.S.Z.12 for more repairs, this time to fix a damaged elevator. On the same day Lieutenant Crump in S.S.Z.20 was escorting a convoy near Rathlin Island when he witnessed a trawler dropping depth charges on a suspected submarine contact. On 16th April Major Irving Hartford made his final sortie as CO, flying to Whitehead in S.S.Z.20, escorting the *Princess Maud*. His successor Major W.Pennefeather carried out a similar duty on 23rd April in the same airship. St George's Day 1918 was also the date of a bold and valiant attempt to deal with the U-boat menace by other means. The plan was to block the enemy's access to the sea from its base at Bruges by blocking the canal mouth at Zeebrugge with sunken warships. One of the blockships was the twenty-eight years old H.M.S. *Thetis*, an *Apollo* Class cruiser of 3400 tons which had previously served as the depot ship at Larne Naval Base. The early patrol that morning had been flown by Lieutenant Crump in S.S.Z.12, who was making his first visit to Bentra. A few days later, on 26th April, he had to land S.S.Z.20 at Larne when the airship's engine developed carburettor trouble.

The UB-85 and the Kempock

On the morning of 30th April the German Type UB III coastal torpedo attack submarine, UB-85, was on patrol off the County Down coast. On sighting the steam coaster *Kempock*, the U-boat surfaced and engaged the target with its 88 mm deck gun, the coaster fought back and a two hour gun battle ensued. UB-85 was in the end victorious but at high cost, as it proved impossible to submerge, so great was the damage caused by the valiant *Kempock*. As the U-boat limped north it ran into HM Sloop *Coreopsis*, on its first patrol out of Belfast. Before long it was the turn of the Korvettkapitan Kerch and his crew

This is the only known image of the UB-85, here shown on the right tied up alongside UB-82 (U-Boot Archiv)

to abandon ship. UB-85 was sunk by gunfire 9 miles east of Blackrock, Islandmagee. For the Germans, the war was over and they were landed at Larne before transfer to a prisoner of war camp. A total of nine U-boats were sunk in the waters around the north and east coasts of Ireland during the war.

Patrol work

On 5th May S.S.Z.12, for a reason that the passage of time has obscured, was on the ground at Bentra when the envelope had to be ripped open for an emergency deflation. The partially dismantled airship was returned by sea from Larne to Luce Bay. It was flying again three days later. Lieutenant Crump in S.S.Z.20 had another taste of naval pyrotechnics on 27th May when he sighted bubbles of oil while escorting the *Princess Maud*. A trawler and a drifter dropped eight depth charges. Not to be left out, he unloaded a couple of 65 lb bombs himself the following day. On 30th May he noted that the inbound convoy, which he overflew for eight hours at a height of 1000 feet, was carrying 35,000 troops from the USA.

The Princess Maud nears harbour escorted by an airship (via Ernie Cromie)

In June 1918 the *Princess Maud* was fitted with self-protection equipment of a rudimentary kind, machine-guns and smoke generating apparatus. A gun crew was also supplied. The Admiralty further instructed the owners that all crossings during the hours of darkness should be made at full speed with no lights showing. In the event the month brought something of a respite when compared to the level of activity during the spring.

July began quite excitingly for Lieutenant Crump. On 4th of the month he was escorting the *Princess Maud* from a height of 3800 feet in S.S.Z.20 when the engine stopped. There was a problem with the crank handle, flywheel and crankshaft. He re-started the engine by kicking the propeller with his foot.

A chart has survived showing the 19 patrols made from Luce Bay during the week ending 13th July. Six round trips were made to Bentra, while patrols along the Ulster coast ranged as far north as Rathlin Island and as far south as St John's Point on Dundrum Bay. One of the pilots had a mishap on 15th July, which the log book entry records laconically with the single word "Wrecked". S.S.Z.12 was coming to the end of a north-western patrol. Having escorted the *Princess Maud* into harbour, the airship altered course to return to Luce Bay and collided with the flag-staff on the West Pier at Stranraer, causing damage to both the car and envelope - which caused quite a sensation among the large crowd of people gathered there. Both crew and airship were back in the air soon.

The Princess Maud with escort in 1917 (Donnie Nelson Collection)

The D.H.6 otherwise known as the Clutching Hand or Orange Box (JM Bruce/GS Leslie Collection)

Two views of the F.E.2b which landed at Bentra (D&N Calwell Collection)
In the top image it would appear that one of the RNAS ground crew is posing in the rear cockpit.

Did Jack Semple fly to Luce Bay to take this picture of a B.E.2e? (D&N Calwell Collection)

Fixed-wing aircraft

The airships were soon to be reinforced by the addition of fixed-wing aircraft in the shape of "A" and "B" Flights of No.255 Squadron, which were equipped with de Havilland D.H.6s and soon became redesignated as No.258 Squadron. They were joined by an additional flight of the same type from No.244 Squadron. These obsolete training aircraft, which were known not altogether affectionately as the "Clutching Hand" or due to its slab-sided appearance, the "Orange Box", were used to patrol the waters up to ten miles off-shore. They could not compare in endurance to the airships and were only a little faster but they did add extra eyes in the sky. As mentioned earlier Harland and Wolff had constructed many D.H.6s and at least one of these, C4430, flew from Luce Bay. It is not known if any of these aircraft landed at Bentra but some aeroplanes undoubtedly did. The airship station had become known locally as "Whitehead Aerodrome" and a photograph exists of an aircraft on the ground there taken by Jack Semple, a keen amateur photographer and nephew of James Long. It is of a bombing type flown by the RFC - the F.E.2b. Its appearance at Bentra presents something of a mystery. The most likely explanation is that it was manufactured by the Glasgow engineering firm, G.&J.Weir and visited Whitehead on an unofficial test flight - perhaps to bring back some good Ulster produce. Jack Semple also took a photograph of a B.E.2e, which was used by the RNAS as a trainer but this is clearly at Luce Bay. However, was Jack Semple flown over there to take his photograph?

On 19th August Lieutenant Crump recorded that he landed S.S.Z.20 at Bentra to replenish his ballast and on 14th September he searched for a sinking ship near the Gobbins Buoy off Islandmagee.

The weather in September turned unpleasant again but ships were still being sunk and

The Met Section at Luce Bay pose with their theodolite and balloon (via Tom Jamison)

patrolling continued. The first combined patrol of two airships and four D.H.6s took place on the last day of the month.

The importance of meteorology

Gilbert Holland Price arrived at Luce Bay at about this time. He had been posted to the Meteorological Section as a junior assistant. Luckily he has left a detailed memoir to posterity. The changeover from RNAS to RAF and the arrival of the D.H.6s had not been entirely trouble free. The new adjutant had been attempting to convert ex-naval residents to a more spit-and-polish based regime, which was resented - as was his desire to ensure that they exchanged their naval uniforms for khaki. The airship and aeroplane pilots tended not to rub along together very well either and made disobliging remarks about each other's aircraft. The new service was not without its teething problems. Price worked in the "Met Hut", where a team provided a twenty-four hours a day service, supplying the raw data on barometric pressure, wind strength and direction, temperature, amount of cloud and rainfall; which was then transmitted by code from all over the UK to the Met Office in London. Synoptic charts were then drawn up and detailed local forecasts sent back for the guidance of flying officers. Additionally, local wind strength at different altitudes was taken by the use of small balloons which were tracked by theodolite as they ascended. At night

Farewell to the airships (Donnie Nelson Collection)

their progress was tracked by means of a small candle suspended from the balloon with a length of twine.

The final days

On 23rd October S.S.Z.11 was in the vicinity of Ballykelly when heavy gunfire was reported. Neither the pilot, Lieutenant Deaker, nor the crew of S.S.Z.12 which was escorting a convoy in the area could find anything amiss. On the same day Lieutenant Crump, flying S.S.Z.20, escorted the *Princess Maud* for the last time before going off for a week's service afloat in H.M.Trawler *Corrie Roy*. In November a bombing attack was made by S.S.Z.12 on a suspicious oil patch on the surface near the Maidens, islands to the north-east of Larne. Armed trawlers joined in and confirmed by hydrophone detection that a submarine was present. No confirmation of a sinking could be made.

Before the war ended plans had been made to introduce a much larger type of airship, the rigid, Zeppelin-type 33-Class, to patrol out into the Atlantic. Preliminary work began on a suitable shed near Lough Neagh but the Armistice was signed before this was completed.

On Monday 11th November 1918 the Armistice was signed and the "war to end all wars" came to its conclusion. By December the airships had ceased to fly and Bentra returned to its rural calm and peaceful obscurity. The farmland was reclaimed and another

51

The Armed Trawler Vera H.960 in Larne Lough - note the 3 pounder gun mounted on the bow (Photograph reproduced with the kind permission of Larne Borough Council Museum Service SH59.1)

farmer, Mr Service, was able to make use of the buildings left behind. Some of the huts were used as holiday homes and later as permanent homes until the late 1950s. As for the *Princess Maud*, she served on until 1932 when she was scrapped following a grounding.

Conclusion

By virtue of its geographical situation and in the light of the technology available at the time, Bentra had played a small but vital part in the network of airship stations which had contributed so importantly to winning the first anti-submarine war. It was a welcome haven for the courageous and skilful airship crews in their frail craft. No doubt they enjoyed the hospitality that the kindly folk of Whitehead and Islandmagee would have given to strangers in their midst. This time has all but passed from living memory, it is important therefore that the exploits of the airmen of Bentra should be recorded for posterity.

In all 147 Submarine-Scout type airships were constructed, 29 with the B.E.2c fuselage, 26 Maurice Farman types, 10 with an Armstrong-Whitworth car, 6 SS-Pushers and 76 S.S.Zeros. No other contemporary aircraft could have performed the jobs the S.S. and S.S.Z. airships undertook. None could match the airships' endurance or slow speed capability. Their deterrent value was immense - during the entire war there was only one instance of a ship being escorted by an airship being sunk. This may be placed in context by considering the fact that of the 12,618,283 tons of merchant shipping lost in the Great War, 11,135,460 tons were sunk by U-boats - 88% of the total. During the final 15 months of the war alone S.S. type airships carried out over 10,000 patrols, flying nearly one and a half million miles in more than 50,000 hours. 49 U-boats were sighted and 27 of these were attacked from the air or by ships. The submarines were kept below the waves, where they used up valuable battery power and were restricted to a speed of only 8 or 9 knots. A brief log entry from a captured U-boat speaks volumes, "Sighted airship - submerged."

A captured German U-Boat, now flying the White Ensign over the Imperial German Navy Ensign, in Larne Lough (Photograph reproduced with the kind permission of Larne Borough Council Museum Service SH59.4)

The author and the Ulster Aviation Society would like to express their sincere thanks to Malcolm and Wesley Johnston of April Sky Design for their excellent work and creative input.

Bibliography

Books

Whitehead the town with no streets by P.J.O'Donnell, Belfast 1998

An Aeronautical History of the Cumbria, Dumfries and Galloway Region Part 2 1915-1930 by Peter Connon, St Patrick's Press, Penrith 1984

Battlebags by Ces Mowthorpe, Alan Sutton 1995

The British Airship at War 1914-1918 by Patrick Abbott, Terence Dalton, Lavenham 1989

Airships by Patrick Abbott, Shire Publications Ltd, Princes Risborough 1991

British Airships in Pictures by Patrick Abbott and Nick Walmsley, Redwood Books, Trowbridge 1998

Recollections of Air Marshal Sir Thomas Elmhirst, privately published, R.T.Elmhirst 1991.

Airship Pilot No.28 by T.B.Williams, William Kimber 1974

The War in the Air by W.Raleigh and A.H.Jones, six volumes, Clarendon Press 1922

The British Rigid Airship 1908-1931 by R.Higham, G.T.Foulis 1961

Zeebrugge by Barry Pitt, Cassell, London 1958

Dreadnought by Robert K Massie, Pimlico, London 2004

The Great War by Winston S Churchill, George Newnes Ltd, London 1933

Army Aviation in Ulster by Guy Warner with Alex Boyd, Colourpoint Books, Newtownards 2004

Belfast International Airport - Aviation at Aldergrove Since 1918 by Guy Warner and Jack Woods, Colourpoint Books, Newtownards 2001

The Innocent Erk - RNAS and RAF Memoirs of Clk 2 Gilbert Holland Price - unpublished manuscript held in the RAF Museum archives.

Articles

Belfast Weekly Telegraph, 30th August 1913

Larne Weekly Telegraph, August 1913

Aerostat Vol.8 No.1 by Air Marshal Sir Thomas Elmhirst, 1977

Wigtown Free Press by Donnie Nelson, 26th June 1986, 18th September 1986, 25th January 1996

Larne Times, 5th September 1986

Galloway Advertiser 24th May 1956, Obituary A.H.Crump

Airships in the war against the U-boats by Robert Jackson, The Rolls-Royce Magazine, September 1992

Ulster Air Mail, January 2004, article by Guy Warner

Official Publications

RNAS Pilot's Flying Log Book - Lieutenant A.H.Crump RAF
RNAS Pilot's Flying Log Book - Flight Sub-Lieutenant B.W.Hemsley RN
Airship Log Book S.S.20
Handbook of S.S.Type Airships. Complied by the Instructional Staff at the Airship Depot,
Wormwood Scrubs, 1917

Websites

www.airshipsonline.com (Airship Heritage Trust)
www.ibiscom.com/sub.htm (U-boat attack 1916)
www.geocities.com (U-boat war 1914-18)
www.gwpda.org/naval (German Admiralty Declaration 4.2.1915 and following events)
www.uboat.net (types of U-boats)
www.rafweb.org (Air of Authority a History of RAF Organisation)

Conversation and correspondence by letter, e-mail and telephone

Mrs Nancy Calwell, Ces Mowthorpe, Patrick Abbott, Mrs Jane Mackie, Tim Elmhirst,
Stuart Leslie, Donnie Nelson, P.J.O'Donnell, Mrs Emma Crocker (Imperial War Museum),
Peter Devitt (RAF Museum), Jerry Shore (FAA Museum), Mark Frost (Dover Museum),
Peter Garth and Den Birchmore (Airship Heritage Trust), John Duggan (Zeppelin Study
Group), Richard Haigh (Rolls-Royce Heritage Trust), Horst Bredow (U-Boat Archive), Joan
Morris, Gemma Reid, and Chrissie Williamson (Larne Museum).